Dedications

I am so extremely grateful to have such a great and supporting family and friends. Without all of you, I would not have this opportunity to create something beautiful through my diction and poetic vision. Thank you all for being here for me, and I have nothing but love for all of you. I love you.

Dino Cook Sr.

Cattima Nicole Millsap

Dino Cook Jr.

Ana Cook

David Cook Sr.

David Cook Jr.

Yvette Campbell

Yvonne Cook

Zelia Cook

Kay Zastrow

Imani Clayton

Raven- Patina- Cook

Dominic Cook

David Cook III

Janet Millsap

Jasmine Hewitt

Samantha Olson

Aryn Mattson

Stephanie Keophiphath

Brandin James

Kelsey Rahn
Kaitlyn Cummings
Anne- Marie Di Cristo

Marvellis Morgan
Kayla Butler
Crystal Richardson
Reigna Perdue
Alicia Lopez
Hadley Kling
Erika Stanley
Sydney Stankowski
Brianna Walker
Suzette Mineau
Laurie Mueller
Maureen Dally
Olivia Bruss
Tony Pham

And so much more; thank you all for everything. I love you dearly.

"prologue"- introduction of the artistic recluse

Sometimes I feel like I'm a dollar bill.
People only want me when they need help.
I'm always bartered with people that trap me in this vault.
I feel like I trap myself in this cage of detachment.
Do you feel like life is the depth of maudlin emotions that makes you stuck?
Ever feel so alone?
Ever feel every bone in your body is exploding like fireworks and breaking piece by piece hearing the bones cracking, echoing loudly in your ears.
The crimson anger and rage appearing through your pupils.
The fear is the fragrance sprayed against your skin.
The whole ideal of the world is messed up, because no one isn't going to care about you.
Time isn't going to stop.

All you have is your tears being the limelight

the darkness as the curtain

My mind is crazy.

I feel like I have an expiration date.

No matter how many mirrors are in front of me, I don't see myself.

My existence

All I see is the fog

The emptiness of the hollowed soul

I always try to postpone the inevitable.

I realize that I've lost control of myself. I classify myself as being lachrymose.

I never want to see my reflection in the mirror.

The somber side of me has all of the control.

I can't even fathom the way my mind is functioning.

I can't sustain myself mentally and emotionally.

I feel like all of my paintings are becoming more tedious.

No synthesis of sublime and extraordinary colors.

It's all pitch black.

My darkness prevents my heart from being tangible by anything that contains nostalgia.

I've been so broken.

I've really lost it.

I'm already drowning in my mortality.

Sometimes, I don't know what I feel and I don't know what I want for myself.

I feel the weight pressing against my lungs.

Suffocation

My mind as become quite ambiguous currently

I've been ambivalent about the emotions that I've been absorbing

I just want some composure

Instead of drinking all of the darkness in the empty glass

The distance hurts

The silence hurts

I can not handle all of the pressure

I feel like my heart is going to burst.

Am I going to go through this bittersweet curse or remain reclusive

Where's the clarity

When will this end

Is the truth out there with the stars

I keep having the same illusion

Causing my heart to become insensible

Then again, my heart has the ability to have constant heartbeats that proliferate

I strongly feel like life and love are tortuous

It makes you stolid

It makes you feel the elation circulate with your human body

Ubiquitous emotions begin to loiter around my head

Films of incomplete canvases transforming themselves replaying and repeating

A realistic delineation

The expression of my emotions that I am currently feeling.

Splattered anger.

Light strokes of happiness and compassion

Flames of my pain enervating me

The sentiment is truly enigmatic

I crave for solace

Possessing the strongest temptation to listen to my heart

Pure silence

My heart and mind are the paradox

Happiness?

The juxtaposition of comfort and love?

To not be alone?

To feel one touch?

Are all of those elements of life classified as being the panacea for the lingering shadows

Maybe there's no remedy

The darkness causes me to decrease my amount of ambition and hope

Which attracts apprehension, causing me to regress to destructive behavior

I can not continue to keep up with my masquerade much longer

Expressing an ounce of vulnerability?

I can not see my own shadow

I see someone's else's instead

I can not observe my own reflection

I see yours

I'm drowning

You already swam to the shore

I am insane for falling to the surface

I am sane for falling to the surface

Help me lose my mind

I was never aware of all of the destruction in my heart

I guess I didn't have a fucking clue

The way you embrace life through your laugh, smile, and appearance brings me to the climax of nostalgia

You do that so flawlessly, with so much grace

You bring my heart alive into human form.

Clouds diffuse the momentum that I always crave

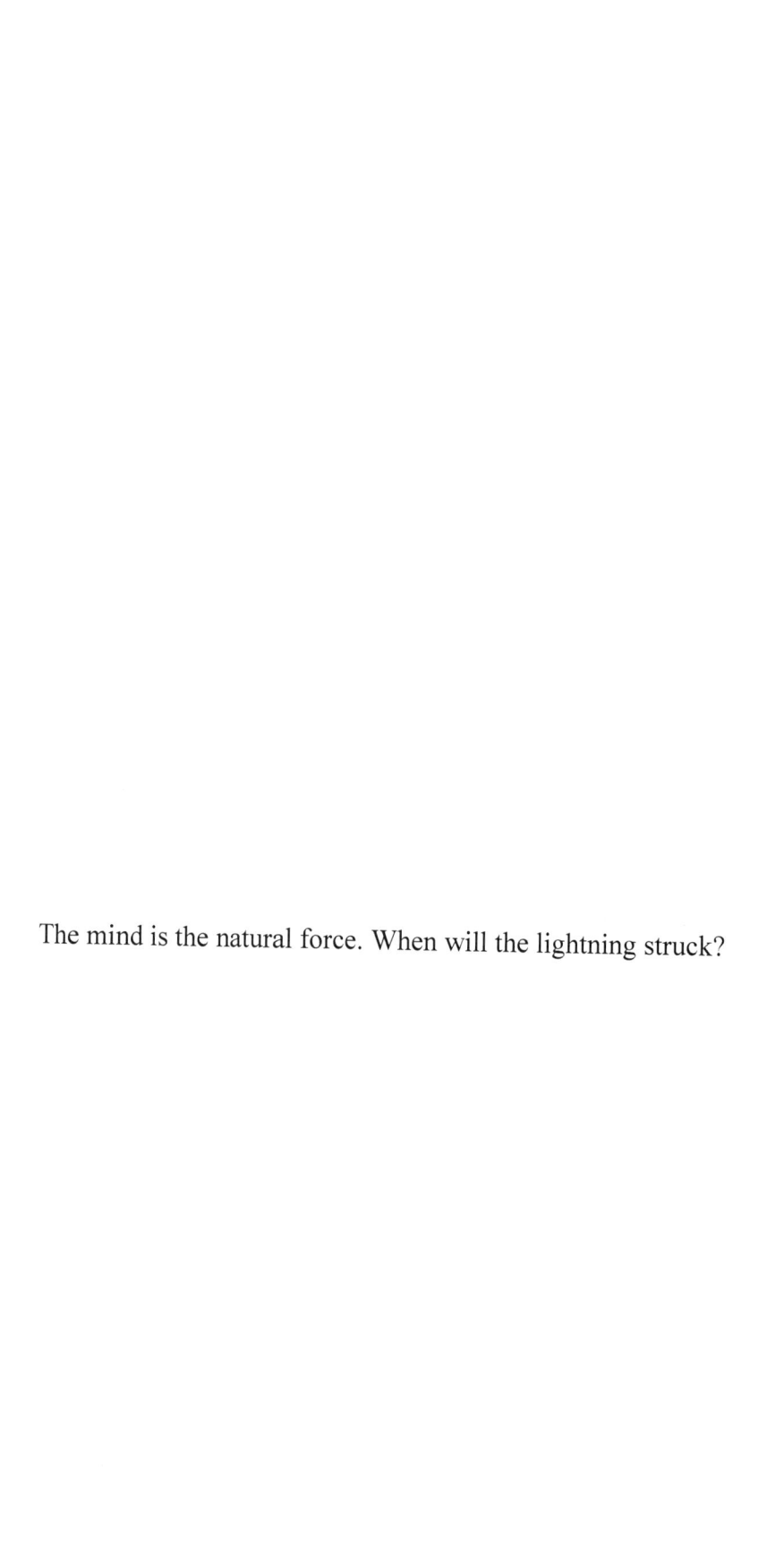

The mind is the natural force. When will the lightning struck?

Abstract senses.

I listen to the same maudlin songs over and over

It symbolizes my languishing constellation

Rainstorms are my weakness and strength

They morph my mindset in a special but abstract way.

The way the rain pours

It's the artistic representation of euthanasia

The way the rain splatters against my skin

It feels like the same way as the blood splatters all over my previous wounds

Over and over again

The way the rain smells

You can inhale the emptiness and distance of melancholy souls

The noise that the rain makes

Each drop of it pounds on my chest

The way it suffocates my every last breath

The way it eradicates and anatomizes the lumps in my throat

I listen to the same maudlin songs over and over.

Abstract senses.

Going up in flames

Pour the gasoline down my body

Burn my existence

Destroy the darkness

Allow the flames to bloom with the ink of my pen

I wrote down the crimson pain and suffering that I've endured

I constantly live in fear

The fear is consuming my flesh

Pour the gasoline down my body

I can smell the disappointment

I can smell the sorrow upon my hands

Allow the flames to rejuvenate every part of me

When I walk around the empty hallways, I never felt so complete in my life

No noise

No people

Just pure silence and the weight of emptiness.

I love that because I feel like my emotions are finally alive

Everything slowly eradicates into particles and dust in my view

Because all I see is you

I want to be able to breathe

To exhale

To live

Without fear

Without the ubiquitous pain and agony

I was a young girl always stuck on the ideology that isolation and detachment was her solution, and those elements can provide her with the love and comfort that she was constantly searching for. Her anger and scream swallowed every part of her. The violence, emotional, verbal abuse, and ignorance that her parents displayed was her mirror, defining her reflection. Their anger and pain within themselves devoured the young girl, and when she displayed an ounce of emotion, they just ignored it, and continued to suppress it. Throughout the years, their hurtful words and actions left her struggling on the ground; leaving her with no momentum and gravity to fly towards her autonomy. Towards a place where she felt like she was enough and happy with every part of herself. She did not have any other outlet to elude from the pain and suffering, so she decided to have the blade and the cuts on her wrist display her worth. The depression and anxiety consumed her flesh, and she allowed it to. Now as an 18 year old, she still continues to struggle with opening up. That's what she does not understand. She can write all of the emotions down on paper or social media sites so fluently and poetically. But when she tries to announce them, it's like her words and voice are her complete blankness of fear. She feels that if her words from her mouth lingered like the scent of the wick of a candle and that the filling fragrance will be overpowering for everyone's senses. She still feels that everything she does or does not do leads to accumulation of darkness, distance, tension, and conflict. In her timeline, it always appeared that way. She has a hard time of letting go. Letting go of the bond with the darkness and fear that has been hindering her from living her life happily. They still consume her and as she expresses her vulnerability, she allows them to consume every hollow part of her, because sometimes she's tired of being strong and holding on to something that she can not obtain. She feels so much guilt and pain for causing so much damage in her pure bonds with her loved ones. She feels so much guilt for covering her emotions with blankets and sheets, but she feels that the only warmth she will ever find is under the blankets and sheets. She has such an altruistic personality. So much love and compassion within her soul and heart. She continues to diffuse love and happiness towards the people she deeply cares about. However, the love and happiness towards the people she deeply cares about. However, the love and happiness are the empty pieces within herself. Then she is left languishing in solitude, pondering about if her existence is worth fighting for. She continues to find the answers.. Even though she feels like she doesn't feel like she can not find them. It is highly difficult to keep fighting, especially when her father told her that life, fear, and time will consume her and that she won't make it. My parents' words and actions were always out of frustration, but that will never justify their behavior. She wants to be something more than the darkness and sadness. She wants to be more than her mental and physical dilapidation. She wants to be happy with herself. I want to accumulate more resilience within myself. There's a lot of pain and fear that has completely changed my self identity and how I define myself as a human being. There's a lot of darkness in this world that has masked my true perspective of life. But I have to pull the curtain and showcase my limelight. I want to tell my parents that this is not me self loathing. This is not me begging for attention. Stop lacking perception, awareness, and discernment. Actually listen and acknowledge me being human. Your pain, ignorance, selfishness, and blindness is going to stop weighing me down. I am free. This is my release. All I want is to recover, and see the brightness shine in my view. I have to continue to fight. I have so many people that provide me with so much warmth and compassion within my frigid soul. I have to fight for them. I have to fight for myself. It hasn't been easy. This is my release.

Mental health is a serious issue that needs to be addressed constantly. Depression, self doubt, anxiety, and so much more can easily consume the mind in a negative manner. Trust me, there were moments that I've allowed the pain to conquer. There were times that I had a deep temptation to end all of the possibilities. Mental health is a serious issue. We have to be here for each other. We really have to bolster each other. We have to make a difference. Every human being deserves to live. We all have the resilience. We just have to help each other with discovering it within. I know the pain feels like it's going to remain within your heart forever. I know that the heart feels like it's failing to function once you allow the pain flow in your bloodstream. I know it feels like you don't have enough power to conquer that pain, and create something beautiful. I've experienced so many events that completely changed my life. I felt like the fog would never clear out of my mind. I began to cope with my emotions negatively, by self-harming, suicide attempts, and so much more. Sometimes I just wanted to let go. I felt that I wasn't enough. I still feel that way sometimes. It's the worst feeling in the world. I've come a long way. I wake up every morning and observe the scars on my wrist. It always takes me back to painful memories. However, it made me realize that throughout high school and college, I wanted to end my life due to what I was fighting against all of these years. But I am still here. Fighting. Accumulating ambition, strength, resilience. It's so difficult. It's easier said than done. I know. It honestly sucks to feel even an ounce of sadness within your heart and mind. And others may think that it's nothing major or say, "Oh they just want attention" No fuck that! Once again, you are so ENTITLED to what you feel regardless of the size of the struggle that you're facing. It's so hard in this world. The amount of love and understanding is diminishing within our atmosphere. The least we can do is diffuse our kindness and compassion. Trust me, I know that I may appear as the positive and strong one, but there are days where I am extremely vulnerable, masking how I truly felt, and etc. However, I realize that I am here for a reason. I am still searching for that reason. You will find that reason. You're so fucking worth it and strong. Never forget that. I'm on this difficult journey with you.

"The Journey with the Artistic Recluse and the Celestial Human Being"

Intoxicating whispers I hear lingering within my mind

My mind's landscape appears to be a nightmare as always

Leaving me hollow and empty

I feel that you feel the same

That's why you are being the wave

Over time, our minds have been eroded by blurred vision

Since you left from my heart, there are many spaces that need to be filled

I want you to know that the pain displayed through my diction is a quiet pain

Internally, the pain is released with insane echoes and screams

The pain is so quiet

The pain is so powerful

The silence is starting to drift with the wind

The roar is unleashed

I wonder everyday how will your presence that lives within my poetry, come alive within my setting again
I wonder if you would question yourself
You may believe that your thoughts and darkness are erupting volcanos
But you are everything to me
You make all aspects of life filled with so much pulchritude
I am honored to be given the opportunity to existing along side of you
I love you

Allow my hands to stroke your ragged edges within your heart back smooth

Allow me to be your poetry

Allow me to imprint my pure devotion on your blank pages of your body

You continue to erase the paragraphs on your skin in order to prevent me from seeing the ink from your pen, dripping like the mascara on your soft and glossy skin

I hope that I can observe your constellation through your coils of leaf brown eyes

I hope I can see your constellation finally shine again

I feel like our hearts will detach in this universe we live in

I feel that our growth as one is postponed

Not able to expand for the better

Our masterpiece was colorful and radiant

It has morphed into an austere, abstruse, and despondent piece of art

I have so much love for her

Hopefully, all the love that I possess can be the paintbrushes stroking our atmosphere with sublime watercolors.

Making everything beautiful again

The purposeful imbalance that every person feels within their minds is love

A powerful element that lifts our souls high in the sky

A powerful element that digs aggressively within our mantles of our hearts

Love is our signature formula

Juxtaposing two auras

Elegantly forming two hearts into one

I love love

The way it's so essential for our human condition

Love fills up my whole world

Without it, my atmosphere would be black and white.

I find it so ravishing and tantalizing that some human beings can get so nostalgic about love

To admire the silence that two human beings diffuse

The core of your mind and heart

A simple touch

A simple kiss

Any representation of true devotion is the force that makes us crave more and more

To cherish it until the end of time

However, love can morph some to become hopeless romantics

The lyric, "the beautiful ones smash the picture." makes so much sense

Love can make some feel like they don't possess enough strength to pull yourself into another's world

It feels like the confusion and ambiguity are the gravitational pull that continues to weigh you down

The confusion is painting your view with rough strokes

And it's causing you to be blind and vulnerable

So vulnerable that you don't have enough strength and clarity within your mind and heart to pull the other person towards your world

You want them to look beyond

And see what love you possess

It feels like you're in the audience watching a play

You see the person closest to your heart in the limelight

Delivering such a captivating performance

But again you find yourself in the audience

Hidden by the darkness and shadows

No matter what, love makes you have this burning desire to have your poetic vision to open the blinds of the other's shadow For your souls to converse To coexist exquisitely

I want to feel our hearts traveling within the shadows
It helps me elude from the pain

Love is a reflecting image of colorful haze

It is so exquisite that it latches onto your heart

It pulls you in

The beauty clearly astounds the human being and provides them with aesthetic pleasure

It feels like you're in a hallucination or apart of reality

It feels like the haze pulls you in closer to spaces that can not be filled

However, you have to remember that haze has two denotations

"A slight obscuration of the lower atmosphere, typically causes by fine suspended particles"

"A state of mental obscurity or confusion"

The question is which of those meanings are your reflecting image of pure devotion

Love is when you lie down on your bed and all you desire is to feel their love
To feel the warmth of their heart through the covers and sheets
You lie on the bed and feel everything falling apart in front of your eyes
And you feel their presence
So redolent
Through the covers and sheets, you feel their warmth and compassion protecting you from sinking into the black void of the depression
You sleep so comfortably, because you always know that they're here

The person you truly cherish are more poetic than any song you truly adore

They're such a mesmerizing rendition of your favorite tracks

I'm perfectly and incredibly blind, because you will always have my heart.

You're anthropocentric
I am just the person with euthanasia
Any human being would classify you as being seraphic
When people see me, I am probably classified as melancholy
I know if someone deeply adored you with all of their heart, they would desire your presence
As long as you and the other individual have each other, your lives would be incessant
Beauty, intelligence, brightness has been congenital for you
Despite all of the sadness you may have, you still have joie de vivre within your radiant heart
I'm just the ocean
You're the waves that erode all of my darkness, so I can actually visualize the kindness and beauty thats in this world

Feeling any special emotion like love or anything for anyone is like being an archaeologist
Digging through your mind to frequently find the vestiges that they left
But then you realize the vestiges are left in the most empty parts of your heart
The person you truly cherish is apart of you
You honestly feel the madness circulating in your veins
You go insane, because you don't have that person sustaining you to remain sane
Don't ever question the veracity of having these emotions
Hold on to them

I don't think I can inhale more of these fumes that the flames are lingering
It is killing my soul
Damaging my wings
The flames are burning all of the scenes that fabricate my dreams
Especially dreams when you say you love me
I'm out of touch
I wish this high can put out these flames
Or should I say, I wish this high can put out this emptiness
The heaviness of the smoke is preventing me from flying above
Is this love?

She pushed herself away from the equation

She thought that was the best solution

The variables will remain unknown

Our illnesses possess more autonomy that's bigger than the both of us
I'm going to continue to tell you that if you close your eyes, you will be able to see the universe internally eventually
I'll be the colors that help brighten your mind
To guide you away from the blindness

I wish it was that simple

I know there's a vacant space between us right now

I wish I could pull you closer and hug you tighter to fill the emptiness

To heal you

I wish it was that simple

There are a lot of reasons why I love her

I could say that I love the way she smiles and laughs

I could say the I love the way she looks at me when we go on car rides

I could say that I love the way she stares through my soul when she enters any room

Don't get me wrong

I love all of those things about her, but I want to go more in depth

I love her brightness and darkness

It shows that she's truly human

A pure and alluring human being

I miss how things were too

But I'm still here as your noise and silence to ease you towards the right direction

We had to dig deeper into our surface in order to find our true purpose

you injected the ink within my heart

i thought i would have this sudden ability to write fluently again

but now my heart is hollow

no comprehension of my own diction

my vision

i have this intense fear of you not being apart of the spaces of my heart

the spaces that i opened up for you, so you had a place to call home

my hands shake because i don't feel your brown, calloused hands intertwining with mine

treating your pain with my devotion

my heart aches for your simple touch

your presence

i tense up when i hear your name, but not your voice

biting on my bottom lip

numb

no expression

now, i only feel the rain pour against my sweet, smooth caramel skin

the precipitation assimilating my agony and heartache

it's cleansing all of the venom

the rain is my rejuvenation

yet, it is my tears that I cannot display

my resilience is hidden in disguise
now the rain will always remain as the warmth upon my skin
the warmth that i will never lose

i will always keep my heart open
i will always have the wounds open
the sun and water can heal it with their natural clarity
i have a huge heart
i feel the "simplest things" so deeply
yes, there's some downfalls to that
Sometimes i question, "Why is that wrong?"
why is it wrong to feel things so deeply and poetically?
to love deeply….
to think deeply…
depth is so important to me
some people may think that depth is dangerous

but in my opinion, depth is a local anesthetic

she's the array of colors that smears reds, blues, yellows within the cracks in my heart
i wonder what will happen when the colors fade?
will she paint another coat?
will she have any colorful colors left within her canvas?
i will never run out of paint
i will never have her be an austere canvas

the thought of letting her go feels impossible

your words

i just began speaking your language so fluently

our time has run out

now i remain speechless

your words now remain as the taste that sizzles on the surface of my tongue your shadow and light are the drifting echoes of the piano's melodies

my heart was loud as a lion's roar, but it was tamed by blurred vision

What is your favorite work of art?

my favorite work of art will always be her

her curves

smile

the shape of her lips and nose

i remember her arms being so smooth

she may believed that they were rough due to her battle scars

displayed

but they were so alluring. and always will be

they showcase her story

it shows her strength

i will adore the atoms that comprised her being

her beautiful brown eyes

i will always remember how her eyes stared down through my soul

i remember how her mouth was fluent with my language

her smile, her luminous, radiant teeth are just so heartwarming and soothing

her clothing always possessed such a fresh scent

it always lingered in the room after she departed

i will always adore how her fingernails ran through her green hair

she was the electric current flowing in my vein, especially when she gave me her full attention

especially when she told me that she loved me

she will always remain as my favorite work of art

I will always love everything about her

her existence will always remain as a masterpiece

she was the masterpiece that completed my unfinished painting

anyone.

anyone can ask me what am i thinking about

anytime of day

any season

my answer will always be her

they wonder and ask why

and my response will always be why not?

she bolstered me to elude from the pitch black void, splattered with white ink

she bolstered me to cherish my own name

to cherish my existence

to cherish the opportunity to be alive

i will always be gratified by her alluring pulchritude

they ask again, "is this your explanation of love?"

my response will always be yes.

love may feel like it will take more than a miracle to obtain

however it gives you all of the gravitation and momentum to float with the clouds

the audience is speechless

but one says, "do you love her?"

my answer

my response

my reply will always be yes

is your love in the center of the eclipse?

your light doesn't blind me anymore

your fog is the murderer of the mind

unfortunately, the fog holds me close

an opening

is love about painting pictures of a war?

each day, i see you less and less

at first you were the sun shining adjacently with the blue colored sky

the clouds continued to drift away with the wind

as days passed by, there was no sunlight

the sky became clearer and clearer

i wondered where the clouds drifted off to

i realized that the clouds were my eyes

they continued to pour and pour.

each day, i see you less and less

i wondered if i was wasting my young years

possessing a heart like a true romantic

having that desire to have our bond being chivalrous

you aren't here

but i feel you up there

now i only see you at night

you are the orange colored sky

i finally see you undressed

naked

you look so beautiful

god i miss you

i hope our skies will coexist

reclaiming our minds, body, and spirit

i wanted you to adventure the poetic fumes in my mind

to assimilate

to inhale

to exhale

i wanted my poetic fumes to feel the tie-dye and glow and dark hallucinations

i wanted my poetic vision to make you reach the zenith of euphoria

i wanted you to find your nirvana

i wanted my poetic fumes to comfort you when you were sleeping alone

when you were feeling like everything was falling apart

i wanted my poetic vision to open the blinds of your shadows

i wanted the poetic vision to make you understand my atmosphere

i hope my poetic vision patched up any painful and ambiguous wounds and cuts you possessed.

intertwine your hands with mine

just one more time

let me guide you to the asymmetrical meaning of love

i observed the blue canvas above me

clouds floating so gracefully

one particular cloud stood out to me

it was structured like the human heart

the heart continued to float freely

other clouds coexisting with the heart

the heart is filled

eventually the heart disassembled

the broken pieces parted their ways within the blue canvas

that's devotion

i literally can't sleep without the lingering thoughts of you
hallucinations
your hand gracefully lying on my face
your eyes glancing towards my eyes and lips
suddenly you reach over and kiss me again and again
our first kiss happened like that

every night i wake up feeling your presence

it still feels so real

hallucinations

that love

the laughter

the smiles

memories alone

i think about it all

i hope those moments are not apart of my hallucinations

i know there may be some vacant spaces right now

i wish i could pull closer to you

to kiss you harder in order to fill the emptiness

i wish it was that simple

there are so many theories about the creation of the universe. i really find the theories so sublime and deeply incredible. I really adore the theory, "big freeze". this theory is about how the universe has a fixed amount of energy. when the energy decreases, the universe begins to have a slower pace due to the particles within the universe when there is a slow loss of heat. isn't that love?

in addition, in 1915, Einstein introduced the revoluntary general theory of relativity. this theory involves with space and time being classified as dynamical quantities that were morphed by the matter and energy in the universe. it's so fucking fascinating that the exposition of the universe made the outstanding discovery of modern cosmology. it is so abnormal how the universe has not existed forever. the universe and time has its exposition in the big bang. however, there's no particular boundary hypotheses on the predication of how the universe will crumble or become dilapidated. the universe and time deeply affects us human beings. especially, when the contracting phase will not possess the opposite arrow of time to the expanding phase. at least according stephen hawking. but it makes so so much sense. it throughly provides a synopsis of how we will continue to become older, and the possibilities of us getting younger is ceases. it deeply explains how time will never go backwards. it will never rewind. isn't that love?

i see the reflection of you in my eyes

your blinding shadows is among the stars

like the moon, you are absolutely beautiful when you're breaking

into different phases

it makes you human

i miss melting with your touch

your fog is the murder to the mind

unfortunately, the fog pulls me close

an opening

is love about painting pictures of a war?

invasion of

you drowned with the faded love

you staying within my heart is perpetually uncomfortable

having pure devotion for you feels like an inconvenience

the roots you planted within my heart continued to grow and grow

the roots tangled my heart and lungs

while you bloomed out of my chest, i was left with bones filled with melted gold

the pain continues to flare up

was loving you so deeply an inconvenience

invasion of

i still feel the gentle soft touch of your fingertips

i still feel the beating of your fists against my heart

unable to pump blood to continue my circulation fluently

unable to function

i continue to walk as a human being

a human being who is dead but yet alive

i still have this quenched thirst to taste your essence

i have to eradicate my addiction

my love for you

as the rain continues to pour

i feel rejuvenated

i feel my rebirth

the raindrops continue to flow on my window panes within my mind

the condensation making everything unclear

i still see the trace of your hands on the window pane

is this apart of my reality or my illusion

crumbled paper is my silent pain

you burned my words with your insensitivity

i pour my heart out for a reason
i have so much love to give

i am letting you go

i am letting you go

i am letting you go

i forgive you

i forgive you

i forgive you

not for you, but for myself

what is your favorite work of art?

her.

her curves, smile, shape of her lips and nose

her arms are so smooth

she may believe that they are rough due to her battle scars displayed

but they're so alluring

it shows her story

it shows her strength

i adore the atoms that comprised her being

her beautiful brown eyes

her eyes stares down through my soul

her mouth is fluent with my language

her smile

her luminous, radiant teeth are just so heartwarming and soothing

her clothing always possesses such a fresh scent

it always lingers in the room after she departs

i adore how her fingernails run through her green hair

she feels like an electric current flowing in my veins

especially when she gives me her full attention and tells me that she loves me

she's my favorite work of art

i love everything about her

her existence will always remain as a masterpiece i will always keep my heart open

i will always have the wounds open

the sun and water can heal the wounds with their natural clarity

i have a huge heart

i feel the simplest things so deeply

yes there's some downfalls to feeling so deeply

but sometimes I question

why is that wrong

to love deeply

to think deeply

depth is so essential

some may feel that depth is dangerous

harmful

but depth is my local anesthetic

do you still have my pillow cover
is your blue ombre curls adjacent with the patterning
what are you wrapping yourself with

warmth

isolation

is your door closed

or is it cracked with perception

do you sleep with your eyes closed or open now

the concrete walls begin to crack as you are slowly slipping from a

reflection where the cracks meet

tears

loneliness lingering in your scars

what are you wrapping yourself with? your skin dilapidated

exposed

all that is left in the bedroom is a skeleton of white bone

so hollow

so pure

the love you were given was the cure

no

no

no

the love was flowing with the rush of warm and fresh air

you did not once grasp onto it

will your walls rebuild

will the cracks of your reflection heal

will you obtain the love within yourself

or remain as a living skeleton lying on a peaceful bed with lingering

shadows

every second

every minute

every hour

i continuously struggle with the thought of you in my heart and mind there's always a place within my heart for you

for warmth

for any kind of love

but now I am at the point where I am autonomous and free

what's more difficult, to have them so close or so far?

it seems like my love is not ripe until its season

being young with a broken heart filled with deep devotion

till now i will wait till my heart is ripe

not with emotion

only with reason

reality vs. hallucinations

our love was like caffeine

both of us consumed it frequently

increased energy consumption

energy traveling through our bloodstreams

who would've thought that we'd burn through it so rapidly?

so sweet like our sugary syrup kisses

leaving an aftertaste of senses of futility

Made in the USA
San Bernardino, CA
11 March 2018